LEAD

— *With the* —

LIMP

A Disruptor's Guide to Authentic Leadership

CASSANDRA L. WILLIAMS

"Lead With The Limp: A Disruptor's Guide to Authentic Leadership "

Copyright © 2025 (Cassandra L. Williams)

Published by: Cassandra Williams Enterprise

Interior Formatting Done by: New Voice Books LLC

Website: thecassandrawilliams.com

ISBN: 979-8-9989136-2-4

Printed in the United States of America

TABLE OF CONTENTS

DEDICATION

You belong at the table.
You are done hiding
You're tired of performing.
And now, you're rising, leading with your scars still showing and your head held high.

You are not disqualified.
You are destined.
You were born to disrupt and anointed to lead with authenticity.

I also want to acknowledge and thank some very special people who have marked my journey:

To my family and friends, my biggest fans. Thank you for loving me through every version of me. Your presence in every season reminded me of God's faithfulness in the earth. It was never by accident: the family I was born into, the schools I attended, the man I married, the son we raised, or the path I walked. Every piece of it was part of the process that brought me here, and I'm grateful for it all.

To my coaches and mentors, your pour has not been in vain. I am the fruit of your obedience, your boldness, and your sacrifice. Thank you for saturating me in truth, calling out my confidence, sharpening my purpose, and challenging me to become. I carry your wisdom with me every time I speak, lead, and rise.

This book is for all of us.
The ones who lead anyway.
Even with the limp.

HOW TO USE THIS GUIDE

A Note from Coach Cassandra L. Williams,
The Life Tactician™

This isn't just a book.
It's a mirror.
A map.
A ministry tool.

Lead With the Limp: A Disruptor's Guide to Authentic Leadership was created for those of us who 'have wrestled with identity, battled perfection, and questioned if our limp disqualifies us from leading. If that's you, welcome home.

This guide is designed to meet you wherever you are on your leadership journey: limping, leading, healing, or rising. Whether you use it personally, in a small group, or alongside a coach or mentor, here's how to get the most out of it:

1.   Read Slowly. Lead Honestly.

Each chapter is meant to be digested, not rushed. You'll find personal stories, biblical revelation, and a prophetic push toward authenticity. Take time to reflect on what resonates and what challenges you. Take special note of any concepts that you feel are repeated.

I.   Engage the Journal Prompts

These aren't filler questions. They're designed to help you confront patterns, name hidden pain, and clarify your leadership posture. Write freely. Cry if needed. Revisit when ready.

II.   Lean Into Tactical Grace

This section isn't an afterthought; it's a toolkit for the private battles you don't always have time to name. Each entry gives you a scripture, a strategy or affirmation, and a prayer to reset your heart and focus. Use it when life hits hard. Use it when leadership gets lonely. Use it often.

III. Pray. Declare. Apply.

Don't just read, speak the prayers and affirmations aloud. Declare the truth until it feels true. Let the Word become your weapon and your recovery.

2. Facilitate, Teach, or Lead Others Through It

This guide is also powerful for:

- *Small groups*
- *Leadership cohorts*
- *Healing circles*
- *Retreats or coaching intensives*

Each section can become a teaching moment or a healing encounter. Feel free to adapt it for the needs of your people, just be sure to lead from your authentic place, not your polished one.

———————————————

Remember:
You don't have to be perfect to be powerful.
You don't need applause to be anointed.
You don't have to hide your limp to lead well.

Lead anyway.
Limp and all.
You were born for this.

PREFACE

Born to Disrupt

"I praise you, for I am fearfully and wonderfully made. Wonderful are your works; my soul knows it very well." Psalm 139:14

This scripture has been a blessing and a curse depending on what season we are talking about in life. For the younger me, it was a hope… a place I desired to obtain. For the more mature me, it is a firm foundation on which I can stand unapologetically, knowing that God doesn't make any mistakes. God doesn't make mistakes… let that sink in for a minute as your mind begins to reflect over your life and all that has ensued. Like me, you are coming to terms with some inherent truths about your journey.

I wasn't born to blend in. I wasn't born to follow the crowd, maintain appearances, or fit neatly into the boxes society loves to build. I was born to disrupt.

From the very beginning, arriving prematurely at just three pounds and spending my first month fighting to survive, I was marked by the call to live differently. To move differently. To lead differently. To walk through life with something the world would call a flaw, but heaven would call favor.

For years, I misunderstood the mark. I thought my limp, the physical one, and the emotional ones hidden deep inside disqualified me from certain tables, certain dreams, and certain victories. I worked hard to hide it, to perfect the parts of me I thought were acceptable. I wore my weight like armor. I led with my accolades instead of my authenticity.

But then God interrupted my striving with a single, piercing question: **"Will you go with the limp?"** Would I stop hiding? Would I stop wishing for another story? Would I dare to see my limp not as my limitation, but as my legacy?

This book is an invitation for you and for me to stop seeing our wounds, imperfections, and disruptions as weaknesses and to start seeing them as ordained. It's a call to *lead with the limp.* Not after we are polished. Not after we are healed. Not after we fit the mold.

Right now. Limping and leading at the same time.

Because the world doesn't need another perfect image. It needs living, breathing, grace-soaked testimonies.

It needs you.

PRELUDE

What Leadership Is,
and What It Isn't

Before we begin, let's tell the truth.

Leadership is one of the most misunderstood assignments on earth. It's not a title. It's not a salary bracket. It's not a perfectly curated life. Leadership is a mantle, a weighty, sometimes invisible burden that calls the imperfect to guide others through valleys they've often had to crawl through first. Leadership is **not** about arriving. It's about showing up consistently, humbly, and often broken.

If you've ever felt disqualified because of your scars, you're not alone. The world celebrates polish and pedigree. But Kingdom leadership is birthed in **pain, process, and obedience.** The kind of leader this book is written for doesn't lead because they have it all together. They lead because they've been trusted with insight forged in fire.

So, let's redefine it:

- Leadership is not perfection. It's permission.
- Leadership is not position. It's posture.
- Leadership is not applause. It's accountability.

"The limp you carry isn't a liability; it's your leverage."

If you're reading this, you're probably a leader already. Not because you declared it, but because the weight you carry won't let you deny it. Does this sound familiar...

- You've carried responsibilities that weren't yours, but you carried them anyway.
- You see patterns in systems and want to fix them.
- You've survived what others were crushed by.
- You feel heavy in rooms where people expect you to be light.
- You can encourage others while battling your own doubts.
- You speak truth even when it's unpopular.
- You feel responsible without a title.
- You've been misunderstood, misjudged, or mishandled, but lead with integrity.

- You hear from God but struggle to explain it.
- You've been called "too much," but feel like not enough.

If you find yourself nodding, welcome. You're not alone, and you're not disqualified. You're exactly the kind of leader this world needs: one who leads limping, not hiding. One who disrupts cycles, not just keeps them running.

Let's go a little deeper.

INTRODUCTION

Breaking Loyal Patterns

For many of us, the real war isn't external, it's internal. It's not about who hurt us. It's about what we agreed to believe about ourselves because of the hurt that we experienced. It's not about the opportunities we missed. It's about why we believed we weren't worthy of them in the first place.

Somewhere along the way, we made unconscious vows:

- Stay small or blend in to stay safe.
- Perform to be accepted.
- Hide your flaws to be worthy of love.

We became loyal not only to people but to survival strategies that no longer serve the people we are becoming. I call these *loyal patterns* ways of thinking, feeling, and moving through life that once protected us but now imprison us.

They tell us:

- Don't step out.
- Don't be seen.
- Don't dare believe that God could use someone like you to disrupt the world for good.

But what if breaking loyal patterns is less about doing and more about becoming? *(Breathe.)* What if true leadership doesn't come from perfect performance, but from authentic surrender? *(Alright, take another breath.)* What if the very thing we think disqualifies us, the limp, the scar, the wound, is the very thing God uses to give us access to the places we were born to influence?

In the pages ahead, you're going to encounter real stories of my own, and those of biblical disruptors like Jacob and Mephibosheth, who dared to wrestle, dared to walk with a limp, and still rose into their calling.

They didn't fit the mold.
They broke it.
And so will you.

Part I: The Wrestle

Where the Limp is Formed

Before the rise comes the wrestle. Before the public breakthrough, the private breaking. Before the mantle, the limp. This is the sacred place where God meets us not to embarrass us, but to wrestle the old out of us so the authentic can emerge.

It's not punishment.
It's preparation.
It's where your limp becomes your legacy.

CHAPTER ONE

The Mark of the Wrestler

I used to believe that success meant arriving without a scratch. That if I prayed hard enough, worked hard enough, looked polished enough, I could erase the evidence of the battles I'd fought. People wouldn't be able to look into my eyes-the window to my soul, and see the pain.

I wanted to be patty perfect just like all the social media reels and photos that I consumed daily, and let my works (accolades, accomplishments) speak for me. But the truth is, the most powerful leaders I know are the ones who walk into rooms marked by the wrestle, by the nights they didn't give up, even when everything in them wanted to.

Jacob was one of those leaders.

Before he became Israel, the father of a nation, Jacob was a man who spent his life striving. Fighting for the blessing. Grasping for validation. He deceived. He manipulated. He ran.

Now this is where many of us would have written Jacob off as unlovable and not worth the effort of redemption...

But on one defining night, Jacob encountered God in a way that would change him forever. He wrestled, not just physically, but spiritually. He wrestled with who he had been and who he was becoming. He refused to let go until he was blessed.

> *Then the man said, "Let me go, for it is daybreak." But Jacob replied, "I will not let you go unless you bless me." Genesis 32:26*

And when the morning came, Jacob had both the blessing *and* the limp. Did you hear that... the blessing (a name change/the favor of God) and the limp. He had the mark of the wrestler. The limp was not a punishment. It was a reminder. A reminder that he had seen God face-to-face and lived. A reminder that he would never walk the same again.

The world says to hide the evidence of your struggle. Heaven says to wear it like a crown so that others may glorify the Father. I didn't realize it back then, but I was living Jacob's story in my own body. Every limp, every ache, every emotional scar carried a testimony, not of failure, but of favor. Not of disqualification, but of *destiny*.

I had fought for my place here. I had wrestled through insecurity, shame, and comparison. I had come face-to-face with my own doubts and fears, and I lived. And though the limp remained, so did the blessing.

Today, I no longer see my limp as a weakness to overcome. I see it as a signal to the world that I have *wrestled* and I have *won*. The blessing is on the broken. The anointing is often found in the ache. And if you dare to stop hiding your limp, if you dare to show up imperfect but present, if you dare to lead while you're still healing…

You'll discover what I did:
You were never disqualified.
You were always destined.

CHAPTER TWO

Carried to the Table: Mephibosheth's Redemption

There are some wounds we walk into, and some we're dropped into. Mephibosheth was just a child when his world changed forever. As the grandson of King Saul and the son of Jonathan, he was born into royalty, destined for influence, leadership, and legacy.

But when tragedy struck and his father and grandfather were killed, fear swept through the palace. His nurse, desperate to save him, scooped him up and fled. In her rush, she dropped him. And from that fall, Mephibosheth was left crippled in both feet from the age of five.

In one moment, everything changed.

Suddenly, the boy who was born for the throne became the man hiding in the shadows. The one once destined for greatness was now living in exile, forgotten and overlooked in a place called *Lo-Debar*, a barren land, a place of no pasture, no promise.

Maybe you know the feeling. Maybe you were dropped, too, not physically, but emotionally. Maybe someone else's fear wounded you. Maybe you carry the aftermath of someone else's brokenness. Maybe, like Mephibosheth, you've settled into a barren place, convinced that your destiny was disqualified because of the fall and the corresponding consequences.

> ***But God never forgets what He promises.***
> ***And neither did David.***

Years after Mephibosheth's fall, David, now king, remembered the covenant he made with Mephibosheth's father, Jonathan. And he asked a question that would change Mephibosheth's life:

> *"Is there anyone still left of the house*
> *of Saul to whom I can show kindness for*
> *Jonathan's sake?" (2 Samuel 9:1)*

The answer was yes.
Broken. Hidden. Limping.
And yet, still chosen.

David summoned Mephibosheth, not to shame him, but to *restore him.* Not to punish him for his condition, but to *seat him at the king's table.* Not as a servant, but as a *son.*

The Bible says that from that day on, Mephibosheth always ate at the king's table, and though he was lame in both feet, he was counted among royalty. And what he couldn't do, there were people set aside to do it for him. His limp didn't disqualify him from the table. It was never about the condition of his feet. It was about the covenant over his life. And the same is true for you.

You might still be limping. You might still be carrying the scars of a fall that wasn't even your fault. But heaven has declared: **You still have a seat at the table.**

You are not an afterthought. You are not a burden. You are not too broken to be called.

You are still royal blood. You are still called by name. You are still invited to sit limp and all at the King's table.

And in the places where others see your limp, God sees your loyalty. He sees the way you kept believing. He sees the way you kept wrestling. He sees the way you kept showing up.

Like Mephibosheth, your story is not over because of the fall. It's just beginning because of the *call*.

You belong at the table.

CHAPTER THREE

Favor in Fragile Places

We are trained to believe that favor looks flawless.

Perfect families.
Perfect résumés.
Perfect bodies.
Perfect faith.

But real favor often finds us in fragile places.

It comes to barren wombs like Sarah's. It visits outcasts like Rahab. It anoints shepherd boys like David. It calls limping leaders like Jacob and Mephibosheth. The world calls fragility weakness.

Heaven calls it opportunity.

God is not intimidated by your brokenness.

He doesn't bypass your wounds to find someone more "qualified." Instead, He sets His favor on those who know they need Him most.

Because the truth is, favor doesn't eliminate the limp; it elevates the limp. It transforms the places of greatest weakness into platforms of greatest testimony. I remember praying fervently: *"God, fix this. Fix me."* I thought healing meant erasing every flaw, smoothing every rough place, strengthening every weak part until nothing remained but perfection. He is coming back for a church without spot, blemish, or wrinkle, right?

But instead of removing my fragility, God clothed it with favor. He showed me that His grace isn't just for the healed, the whole, or the strong. His grace is for the limping leader. The bruised believer. The disruptive daughter who doesn't walk like everyone else.

In 2 Corinthians 12:9, Paul heard God say it plainly: *"My grace is sufficient for you, for My power is made perfect in weakness."* Perfect in weakness. What a disruptive idea.

The very areas I tried so hard to hide became the very places God chose to show Himself strong. And here's the wild, beautiful truth: People aren't drawn to your polished image. They're drawn to your *real testimony.* The world is desperate for leaders who are honest about the wrestling. For women and men who don't pretend to have it all together, but who stand up limp and all, and say, *"Look what God has done through me anyway."*

Favor doesn't skip fragile places.
Favor *finds* them.
And favors *them.*

Reflection Questions

1. Where have I equated God's favor with personal perfection?
2. What "fragile places" in my life might actually be invitations for God's strength to shine?
3. What would it look like for me to lead from authenticity, not image?

_____

_____

_____

_____

_____

_____

_____

_____

_____

_____

_____

_____

_____

_____

_____

_____

_____

_____

_____

LEAD WITH THE LIMP

CASSANDRA L. WILLIAMS

_____
_____
_____
_____
_____
_____
_____
_____
_____
_____
_____
_____
_____
_____
_____
_____
_____
_____
_____
_____
_____
_____
_____
_____
_____
_____
_____

Part II: The Unmasking

Where Image, Perfection, and Hiding Lose Their Grip

There comes a moment when God no longer allows the mask to fit. When the weight of hiding becomes heavier than the risk of being seen. Where the old version of you is no longer enough for the places God is calling you into.

This is the part where you must choose:
Image or authenticity.
Perfection or presence.
Optics or obedience.

This is the unmasking.

CHAPTER FOUR

When Image Becomes an Idol

*The Dangerous Pursuit of Looking
Whole While Feeling Broken*

There's a subtle yet dangerous shift that happens when we stop being and start performing. When the focus turns from authentic living to carefully curated appearances. When we trade obedience for optics. When the goal becomes looking the part instead of living on purpose.

That shift is called *idolatry*, and in today's image-obsessed culture, it often comes disguised as self-branding, ministry success, or personal development. It wears flawless makeup, rehearsed smiles, and posts daily on social media, convincing the world and ourselves that if we can just look whole, maybe we won't have to confront the places we feel fractured.

But God doesn't bless masks.
He blesses authenticity.

The most dangerous idols are not statues of gold. They are the ones we quietly erect in the unseen places of our heart:

- The idol of applause.
- The idol of success.
- The idol of status.
- The idol of self-preservation.
- The idol of control.
- The idol of "having it all together."
- The idol of knowing better than everyone else.

These idols keep us from intimacy with God because they make us worship the image we want others to see instead of surrendering the truth of who we really are. *Jacob is a perfect example.* In his desperation for validation, Jacob put on Esau's clothes. He disguised his voice. He covered his smooth skin with goat hair to feel like his brother. He performed his way into a blessing, but it came at the cost of living under the weight of deception. He spent years running, hiding, manipulating, and surviving. But when God wrestled him in the dark, all of Jacob's props were stripped away.

No costumes.
No disguises.
No audience.

Just Jacob. Limping. Wounded. Exposed.

It was there in that raw, honest space that Jacob was finally renamed Israel. Not because of who he pretended to be, but because of who he finally *became.* Mephibosheth also wore an invisible mask. Though physically crippled, his greater injury was to his identity. He saw himself as a "dead dog," unworthy of honor, unworthy of the king's table. But David didn't call for Mephibosheth because of what he could perform. He called him because of *who he was, by covenant,* an heir. Even when Mephibosheth tried to disqualify himself, David restored him.

And yet, how often do we do the same? We build platforms for God while hiding our real selves from Him. We lead others while quietly nursing our brokenness behind closed doors. We settle for image worship, where the version of us on the outside becomes more important than the restoration God wants to do on the inside.

But true leadership, true healing, and true wholeness demand honesty. You don't have to perform for God. You don't have to wear Esau's clothes. You don't have to prove your worthiness at the king's table. You just have to show up, limping, wounded, real. Because *God restores what we reveal.* He cannot heal what we refuse to bring into the light. The greatest freedom comes not from curating your life to look whole, but from letting God make you whole from the inside out.

Reflection Questions

1. What parts of your life have become more about image, titles, or optics than authentic, purpose-driven living?
2. What idols, whether success, applause, or perfection, have you erected that keep you from showing up honestly before God and others?
3. How has performance-based living affected your relationship with yourself, with God, and with others?
4. In what area of your life is God calling you to take off the mask, dismantle the idol, and show up as your authentic self?
5. What would it look like for you to live limping but liberated instead of hiding and bound?

_____
_____
_____
_____
_____
_____
_____
_____
_____
_____
_____
_____

LEAD WITH THE LIMP

_____

_____

_____

_____

_____

_____

_____

_____

_____

_____

_____

_____

_____

_____

_____

_____

_____

_____

_____

_____

_____

_____

_____

_____

_____

_____

_____

_____

CASSANDRA L. WILLIAMS

LEAD WITH THE LIMP

_____

_____

_____

_____

_____

_____

_____

_____

_____

_____

_____

_____

_____

_____

_____

_____

_____

_____

_____

_____

_____

_____

_____

_____

_____

_____

_____

CHAPTER FIVE

The Cost of Hiding

*How Fading to the Background
Can Shrink Your Destiny*

We often think of a limp as something we can see. A physical impairment that causes a person to walk differently, slower, or with visible struggle. But what about the limps we can't see? The ones that reside deep within the heart, hidden behind smiles, titles, and accomplishments? These are the emotional and spiritual limps, disappointments, betrayals, and unresolved traumas that cause us to hide in plain sight.

Yes, you heard me. We can be leading in the boardroom, showing up on social media, serving in ministry, or parenting with excellence, and still be limping. We show up, but not fully. We engage, but with walls up. We offer support to others while secretly wishing someone would notice the crack in our armor.

It's easy to dismiss these internal wounds because they don't demand attention like a physical injury does. No crutches. No cast. No visible scars. Yet they shape the way we see ourselves, God, and the world around us. They make us shrink back, play small, or worse, overcompensate with perfectionism and people-pleasing.

The truth is, many of us are experts at hiding in plain sight. We know how to show up polished, prepared, and performing, while the inner version of us sits in a corner, fearful of being found out. We've convinced ourselves that if we keep busy, keep achieving, and keep pretending, no one will notice the limp. But God sees. He always sees.

It's safer in the background.
Fewer eyes.
Fewer opinions.
Less risk.
But also…less impact.
Less obedience.
Less fulfillment.

There's a unique pain that comes from knowing you were called to lead but choosing to shrink instead. A suffocating ache that whispers, *"Stay small. Blend in. Don't make waves."*

It's the internal conflict of knowing there's more inside, more ideas, more influence, more authority, but staying silent so you don't stir discomfort, criticism, or rejection. It's not always loud rebellion. Sometimes it's quiet resignation. And while you may look strong, composed, and successful on the outside, inwardly, you're limping.

Like Mephibosheth in Lo-Debar, many of us hide in emotional and spiritual wastelands, convinced we're no longer worthy of being seen, heard, or valued. Mephibosheth, the grandson of King Saul, once sat in royal places. But after tragedy struck, leaving him both orphaned and crippled, he was dropped literally and figuratively into obscurity.

Lo-Debar wasn't just a physical place; it was a prophetic representation of how we retreat into barren places when life breaks us. No pasture. No significance. He lived hidden in plain sight, alive, but not truly living. Existing, but not flourishing.

And isn't that what many of us do?
We show up to work. We show up at church. We show up for others. But inside, we've set up residence in Lo-Debar, convinced that because of our limp, our shame, our past, our pain, we no longer have a seat at the table. But hear this: **God isn't calling you out to embarrass you; He's calling you out to restore you.**

David sent for Mephibosheth, not to punish him or remind him of his brokenness, but to restore him to the king's table. To return him to his rightful place of honor, inheritance, and belonging. Every time you hide, you rob the world of the light you carry. Every time you fade back, you delay the lives your voice could transform. Every time you say, *"I'm not enough,"* you argue with the One who called you.

You were never created to dim your light for the comfort of others. You were created to disrupt darkness.

The cost of hiding isn't just your own stagnation; it's the stifling of your assignment. The impact of your voice. The legacy of your leadership. The lives assigned to your obedience. God is still sending for those hiding in Lo-Debar. He's still calling for the limping leaders. The ones who feel overlooked. The ones who limp in secret behind the masks of perfection. And He's saying, *"Come out. You still belong at the table."*

Reflection Questions

1. Where have you been hiding in plain sight?
2. Can you identify your personal Lo-Debar, a place of isolation, fear, or shame where you've settled? What has it cost you emotionally, spiritually, and relationally?
3. What are you afraid will happen if you let yourself be fully seen?
4. What would restoration look like for you if you allowed God to call you back to the table?

_____

_____

_____

_____

_____

_____

_____

_____

_____

_____

_____

_____

_____

_____

_____

_____

LEAD WITH THE LIMP

_____
_____
_____
_____
_____
_____
_____
_____
_____
_____
_____
_____
_____
_____
_____
_____
_____
_____
_____
_____
_____
_____
_____
_____
_____
_____
_____
_____
_____
_____

CASSANDRA L. WILLIAMS

LEAD WITH THE LIMP

_____

_____

_____

_____

_____

_____

_____

_____

_____

_____

_____

_____

_____

_____

_____

_____

_____

_____

_____

_____

_____

_____

_____

_____

_____

_____

_____

_____

CHAPTER SIX

The Myth of Perfection

Trading Pressure for Peace

Perfection is a moving target. Just when you think you've hit it, the standard shifts again. You lose the weight, then it's your skin. You fix your tone, then it's your posture. You lead the meeting, then it's your delivery.

It's exhausting, isn't it? And yet, many of us have unknowingly enrolled in this never-ending race toward an invisible finish line. We bought the lie that if we could just get it all right look right, talk right, perform right, then maybe, just maybe, we'd finally be worthy, safe, or accepted.

But that's the deception of perfectionism.

It promises freedom but delivers bondage. It tells us: "You're never enough. Try harder. Do more. Look better." But the truth of grace says, "You're already chosen. Already loved. Already enough."

Perfectionism is not just a mindset; it becomes a spiritual limp that keeps us hiding behind performance. It whispers that your value is tied to your flawless execution, your image, and your accomplishments. It convinces you that resting is lazy, mistakes are fatal, and vulnerability is weakness.

But here's how to identify perfectionism when it's silently running your life:

- You set unrealistic, often unattainable standards for yourself and others.
- You tie your worth to your work, feeling like a failure if you don't perform flawlessly.
- You procrastinate not because you're lazy, but because you fear not doing it "perfect enough."
- You avoid trying new things unless you're sure you can master them.
- You obsess over other people's opinions, replaying conversations, and criticizing yourself for what you should have said or done.
- You feel uncomfortable when things are "good enough" because you equate peace with laziness.

- You struggle to celebrate progress, always moving the goalpost further away.

Perfectionism is sneaky because it looks like excellence, but it's driven by fear, not faith. It's about control, not surrender. It's about self-reliance, not grace.

But Jesus never asked us to be flawless. He asked us to follow. Even with the limp. Especially with the limp.

Because where the world values polish, God values presence. The world claps for the perfect performance, but God draws near to the humble heart. The world celebrates filters and facades, but God moves through cracks and weaknesses.

The more you rest in who you are, not who you think you should be, the more space He has to work through you. Your limp doesn't disqualify you; it actually becomes the place where His grace shines brightest. Paul said it best in 2 Corinthians 12:9: *"My grace is sufficient for you, for my power is made perfect in weakness."*

Perfectionism will drain your peace, distort your purpose, and delay your progress. But when you lay down the idol of perfection, you pick up the gift of peace. You trade pressure for peace. You allow God to use the real you, not the rehearsed you.

That's where freedom lives.

Reflection Questions

1. What "perfection lies" have you unknowingly accepted as truth about yourself or your life?
2. How has perfectionism shaped your behavior, pace, and inner dialogue?
3. In what ways has perfectionism robbed you of peace, joy, and authenticity?
4. What truths about God's grace and sufficiency do you need to embrace today?
5. Where is God inviting you to release control and follow Him, limp and all?

_____

_____

_____

_____

_____

_____

_____

_____

_____

_____

_____

_____

_____

_____

_____

_____

LEAD WITH THE LIMP

CASSANDRA L. WILLIAMS

Part III: The Rise

Grace to Disrupt, Lead, and Build Legacy

The wrestle marked you.
The unmasking stripped you.
Now comes the rise.

But this rise isn't into perfection, it's into presence. It's not about building platforms; it's about building legacy. It's not about thriving by the world's standards; it's about disrupting, transforming, and leading with the limp.

This is the rise of:
The limping leader.
The disruptor.
The legacy builder.

CHAPTER SEVEN

Grace for the Limping Leader

When You're Called to Lead Before You Feel Whole

What happens when God calls you forward while you're still healing? When you're still unsure, still aching, still not fully "together"? That's the weighty, uncomfortable space where *grace meets calling*.

Throughout Scripture, God consistently uses the unqualified, the overlooked, and the broken. Moses had a stutter. David had a scandal. Esther had a secret. And yet, all of them were called, anointed, and positioned to lead.

But let's be honest, there are moments when the limp feels louder than the call. When your insecurities whisper, *"You can't lead like this."* When past failures stand at the door of your future and say, *"You're disqualified."* When the ache of what's unhealed makes you want to retreat instead of rise.

That's what keeps many leaders stuck in hesitation, holding back their gifts, shrinking their voice, and sitting on their assignments. We assume God is waiting for us to feel whole before we lead boldly. But He's not. He's waiting for us to trust His grace in the places we still feel broken.

Romans 8:29-30 reminds us of this powerful truth: *"For those God foreknew he also predestined to be conformed to the image of his Son…And those he predestined, he also called; those he called, he also justified; those he justified, he also glorified."*

God is not surprised by your limp. He factored in your wounds, your missteps, your insecurities when He called you. He predestined you, knowing you would limp. He called you, knowing you'd have scars. He justified you, covering you in righteousness, not because of your perfection but because of His love. **And He promises to glorify Himself through your imperfections, not around them.** This is the scandalous beauty of grace: Where we see brokenness, God sees opportunity. Where we feel weak, God shows up strong.

Leadership isn't about perfection. It's about obedience. It's about showing up limp and all and letting your life say, "Even now, God can use me."

You're not behind.
You're not too broken.
You're not disqualified.
You're **graced to lead.**

But to embrace this, you'll have to confront the voices that tell you otherwise:

- The voice of comparison that says others are more qualified.
- The voice of shame that says you should sit down because of your past.
- The voice of fear that says if people see your limp, they'll no longer follow you.
- The voice of perfectionism that says, unless you have it all together, you're not worthy to lead.

All lies.
All distractions are sent to delay your obedience.

Grace silences those voices. Grace gives you permission to lead, even while you're still limping toward wholeness. Grace whispers, *"I knew who you were when I called you. I factored in the limp. You don't lead because you're flawless. You lead because you're chosen."*

So, take your limp, your scars, your lessons, your vulnerability, and lead anyway. The world doesn't need perfect leaders. It needs honest, limping, grace-soaked leaders who point to a perfect God.

Reflection Questions

1. What makes you hesitate to lead right now?
2. What fears, insecurities, or lies are causing you to pull back from your assignment?
3. Where has God already equipped and justified you, even if you still feel unready?
4. What does it look like for you to lead with transparency and grace instead of perfection and performance?
5. How can Romans 8:29-30 become a daily reminder that you are called justified and graced, even with the limp?

_____
_____
_____
_____
_____
_____
_____
_____
_____
_____
_____
_____
_____
_____
_____
_____

LEAD WITH THE LIMP

_____

_____

_____

_____

_____

_____

_____

_____

_____

_____

_____

_____

_____

_____

_____

_____

_____

_____

_____

_____

_____

_____

_____

_____

_____

_____

_____

LEAD WITH THE LIMP

_____

_____

_____

_____

_____

_____

_____

_____

_____

_____

_____

_____

_____

_____

_____

_____

_____

_____

_____

_____

_____

_____

_____

_____

_____

_____

_____

_____

CHAPTER EIGHT

Born to Disrupt

Challenging the Mold and Making Room for Truth

You were never meant to fit in. You were born to *disrupt*; to interrupt the norm, to question the status quo, to challenge the patterns that keep people bound, and to carry a different kind of authority. And that makes people uncomfortable. But it also makes things shift.

Disruptors don't just lead within systems; they challenge them. Disruptors don't just play the role; they redefine the rules. Disruptors aren't concerned with popularity; they're committed to purpose.

Jesus was the greatest disruptor to ever walk the earth. He didn't come to blend in. He came to stand out. He didn't come to maintain broken systems. He came to overturn them. He flipped tables in the temple, not because He hated order, but because the order had become corrupted. He healed on the Sabbath, not to be rebellious, but to restore what religion had made inaccessible. He sat with sinners, tax collectors, and the overlooked, not to dilute truth, but to embody it.

Jesus didn't avoid confrontation. He walked straight into it with authority, love, and boldness. He didn't compromise His message for acceptance. He was so disruptive that systems of power conspired to kill Him. But what they failed to understand is that **disruption is the doorway to destiny.** And so is your difference.

I know this intimately because I spent years shrinking, silencing myself, and trying to lead from a place that looked acceptable but wasn't authentic. I thought if I played it safe, said the right things, and avoided rocking the boat, I could lead without confrontation. But the truth was, I wasn't leading. I was managing perceptions, not stewarding purpose. It took seasons of heartbreak, disappointment, and God stripping me of the masks I wore to finally see I was not created to blend in. I was born to disrupt.

Disrupt the lies that say women like me can't lead with authority. Disrupt the patterns of brokenness that keep families stuck in cycles. Disrupt the systems even in the church that prize performance over healing. The pain of being misunderstood, overlooked, or even rejected comes with the territory of being a disruptor. But so does the privilege of making space for truth to breathe again.

Your difference is divine.
It's not a liability, it's your leverage.
You may not walk like everyone else.
You may not sound like everyone else.
You may not build like everyone else.
That's the point.

The world needs disruptors who will:

- Challenge cultural norms that silence truth.
- Interrupt family patterns that keep people stuck.
- Break religious rules that keep people bound.
- Create safe spaces for others to heal.
- Tell the hard truth in love, even when it's unpopular.
- Confront injustice, not just post about it.

Characteristics of a Disruptor:

1. Boldness in the face of resistance.
2. Compassion that sees the overlooked.
3. Conviction that refuses to compromise truth.
4. Creativity that reimagines systems.
5. Resilience to stand when others walk away.

You don't disrupt for applause; you disrupt for alignment with Heaven's agenda. You disrupt to make room for God's truth in places that have grown complacent. You disrupt because you've seen the other side of comfort zones and know what's at stake.

So, stop shrinking.
Stop apologizing.
Stop waiting for permission.

> *"You were born to disrupt,*
> *and disruptors change the world."*

Reflection Questions

1. What cultural, family, religious, or internal expectations are you being called to disrupt?
2. Where have you been shrinking or silencing your voice to maintain peace at the cost of purpose?
3. What does it look like for you to lead boldly and unapologetically with your difference?
4. How can you lean into the characteristics of a disruptor, even when it feels uncomfortable or costly?
5. Where is God inviting you to flip tables, speak truth, and create room for healing and restoration in your sphere of influence?

_____

_____

_____

_____

_____

_____

_____

_____

_____

_____

_____

_____

_____

LEAD WITH THE LIMP

CASSANDRA L. WILLIAMS

_____

_____

_____

_____

_____

_____

_____

_____

_____

_____

_____

_____

_____

_____

_____

_____

_____

_____

_____

_____

_____

_____

_____

_____

_____

_____

_____

_____

_____

LEAD WITH THE LIMP

_____

_____

_____

_____

_____

_____

_____

_____

_____

_____

_____

_____

_____

_____

_____

_____

_____

_____

_____

_____

_____

_____

_____

_____

_____

_____

_____

CHAPTER NINE

From Surviving to Disrupting

Creating a Legacy of Authentic Leadership

You've survived what others didn't even know you were going through.
You've carried weight in silence.
You've performed while privately wrestling.
You've smiled while secretly suffocating.

But now...
It's time to rise.

Not just for you, but for everyone watching you. For the daughters, the teams, the clients, the congregations, the ones God has divinely assigned to your obedience. Your healing becomes a map for someone else's freedom. Your limp becomes a language of permission. Every scar becomes an invitation for others to stop hiding and start healing.

This is not just about you becoming whole.
This is about you creating a legacy
of authentic leadership.

Because when you lead with the limp, you normalize authenticity. You create space for others to breathe, to break, and to become. You model what it looks like to stand boldly in grace, not perfection. You challenge the cultural and internal expectations that say leaders must be flawless, untouchable, or always polished.

The world will tell you: "Just survive. Just thrive. Just succeed on your terms." But God is calling you to something greater than thriving. He's calling you to transform. To disrupt. To leave legacy.

The world's version of thriving is personal success, more influence, more wealth, more comfort. But God's vision for you is kingdom impact, more souls, more freedom, more restoration. The world says, *"Get yours and protect your peace."* God says, *"Give yourself away. Be a vessel of My power and presence in the earth."*

Thriving without purpose is empty. Thriving without obedience is dangerous. But when you thrive from a place of assignment, authenticity, and authority, your life becomes a conduit of heaven on earth. Jesus thrived, but not by the world's standards. He didn't come to gather followers; He came to make disciples. He didn't build an empire; He established a Kingdom. He didn't preserve His life; He laid it down. And He calls us to do the same. To disrupt, to dismantle, to build, to love, to lead, with the limp, with the scars, with the lessons.

You were born to disrupt.
To break cycles.
To challenge the rules.
To introduce Kingdom culture.
To build new tables where the limping, the overlooked, and the misfits are welcomed.

Your leadership is the seed of your legacy.
Not because you're perfect, but because you're present.
Because you dare to show up as your authentic self.
Because you let your limp be seen and still lead anyway.

That is how legacies are born.
That is how leaders are made.
That is how worlds are changed.

So don't settle for just thriving.
Thrive on purpose.
Disrupt on purpose.
Lead on purpose.
And leave a legacy that outlives you.

Reflection Questions

1. What weights, lies, or masks are you still carrying that it's time to release so you can rise and lead boldly?

2. Where have you been settling for personal thriving, but neglecting the greater call to disrupt, transform, and lead others into freedom?

3. How can your story of survival, healing, and disruption become a blueprint for someone else's breakthrough?

4. What does legacy look like to you, not just for your life, but for the lives God has assigned to your obedience?

5. In what areas is God challenging you to stop playing safe, stop shrinking, and step fully into your disruptive leadership anointing, even with the limp?

_____

_____

_____

_____

_____

_____

_____

_____

_____

_____

CASSANDRA L. WILLIAMS

_____
_____
_____
_____
_____
_____
_____
_____
_____
_____
_____
_____
_____
_____
_____
_____
_____
_____
_____
_____
_____
_____
_____
_____
_____
_____
_____
_____
_____

CASSANDRA L. WILLIAMS

CONCLUSION

Lead Anyway

Even with the Limp. Especially with the Limp.

Even if you're still limping.
Even if you're still healing.
Even if you're still unsure.

Lead anyway.

Because the mark you carry is not your shame, it's your story. It's the evidence that you *wrestled and lived*. That you *got back up*. That you *refused to stay hidden in Lo-Debar*. That you heard the King call your name, and you dared to take your place at the table.

Like **Jacob**, you wrestled with your identity, your fear, and your past. And you walked away, limping, yes, but *renamed*. No longer the deceiver. Now, a nation-builder. The limp didn't disqualify you. It marked the moment your destiny began.

Like **Mephibosheth**, you thought you were discarded crippled by what dropped you. But the covenant still stood. You were still royalty. You were still called. And when restoration came, it came with *a seat at the King's table*, not as a servant, but as a son.

Like **Jesus**, your leadership will disrupt. Not through performance, but presence. Not with perfection, but with power. You will flip tables, confront injustice, elevate the overlooked, and redefine what holy looks like. He led with nail-pierced hands and a resurrected body that *still carried scars*. Your scars don't cancel your leadership. They confirm it.

And like the **caterpillar**, what's developing in you is already in you. Every ounce of strength, wisdom, anointing, and grace you'll need to rise, it's already been encoded in your design. But you must *complete the process*. You may not feel as graceful as the butterfly yet, but you are *just as majestic*. Because transformation is not about appearance, it's about alignment.

You were never called to simply survive.
You were never called to thrive quietly.
You were *called to disrupt boldly*.

To lead with honesty.
To serve with compassion.
To build legacy with your limp still visible.

The world will try to seduce you into polish and performance.
To shrink your voice.
To airbrush your truth.
To stay inside the lines.

But Heaven is sending you as a disruptor, *limp and all,* To color outside the lines, To challenge the status quo, To introduce a new normal where *brokenness and leadership can coexist.*

You are the limping leader.
You are the blueprint.
You are the disruptor.
You are the legacy builder.

And it starts now.

Stop waiting for perfect conditions.
Stop waiting for the applause of people.
Stop waiting to feel ready.

Lead anyway.
Disrupt anyway.
Heal anyway.
Speak anyway.
Build anyway.

Because someone is waiting for you to go first. And when you do, you won't just survive, you'll lead, disrupt, and leave a legacy that shakes systems and transforms lives.

Even with the limp.
Especially with the limp.
You were born for this.

LEGACY PRAYER

Father,

I thank You for every limp, every scar, every moment that tried to take me out, but didn't. I thank You that what tried to break me is now the evidence that You sustained me. I thank You that my limp is not a sign of defeat, it's a sign that I survived, and I am still standing.

Today, I release the weight of perfection. I lay down the idol of image. I silence the voices that told me I had to have it all together before I could lead, love, serve, or show up.

I repent for the places I have hidden behind my limp instead of leading with it. I repent for shrinking when You called me to rise. I repent for surviving when You called me to disrupt.

Now, by Your grace, I step into the call. Even if I limp. Even if I still ache. Even if I'm still healing.

I say **YES** to leading anyway. I say **YES** to disrupting cycles, breaking chains, challenging norms, and building new tables. I say **YES** to being a blueprint for authenticity, a voice for the voiceless, and a safe place for others to see what real leadership looks like.

I declare that I will no longer settle for surviving or even just thriving. I will lead, disrupt, and leave a legacy that shakes systems and makes room for others to walk in freedom.

I accept the mantle of the limping leader.
I accept the mantle of the disruptor.
I accept the mantle of the legacy builder.

Holy Spirit, fill every broken space. Use every scar as a testimony. Empower me to lead, not from perfection, but from Your presence.

I was born to disrupt.
I was born to build.
I was born to lead.
Even with the limp.
Especially with the limp.
And I will do so boldly, for Your glory alone.

In Jesus' name, Amen.

LEAD WITH THE LIMP
DECLARATION

A Manifesto for the Limping Leader, the Disruptor, and the Legacy Builder

I am a limping leader.
I am a disruptor.
I am a legacy builder.

I was never created to fit in. I was born to disrupt. I am anointed to challenge the status quo. I am graced to confront what others avoid. I carry a mantle to break cycles, open blind eyes, and usher in truth where deception once ruled.

I reject the lie that I must have it all together before I can lead. I release the weight of perfection. I lay down the idol of image. I silence the voices that told me to shrink, hide, and play it safe.

I declare that my limp is not my liability; it is my leverage. It is not my shame, it is my story. It is not my disqualification; it is my demonstration of grace.

Like Jacob, I wrestled, and I walked away with a limp and a new name. Like Mephibosheth, I will no longer sit in Lo-Debar. I will take my place at the King's table. Like Jesus, I will disrupt, confront, love, build, and create legacy.

I will no longer settle for surviving.
I will no longer settle for personal thriving alone.
I will lead, disrupt, transform, and leave a legacy that shakes systems and changes lives.

I will flip tables when necessary.
I will create new rooms where the broken are welcome.
I will disrupt patterns that keep others bound.
I will make space for truth, healing, and legacy.

I am not waiting for permission; I have been commissioned.
I am not defined by my limp; I am propelled by my calling.
I am not disqualified by my past; I am qualified by grace.

I am a limping leader.
I am a Kingdom disruptor.
I am the blueprint.
I am the legacy builder.

I will lead anyway.
I will disrupt anyway.
I will heal anyway.

I will speak anyway.
I will build anyway.

Even if I limp.
Especially because I limp.
I was born for this.

Bonus Chapter

Jesus Wept, and So Can You

WHEN THE SON OF GOD FELT

Leadership often demands strength, clarity, and consistency, but what happens when you feel overwhelmed, unseen, or emotionally undone? We tend to compartmentalize our emotions to meet expectations. But Jesus never denied His feelings. He felt deeply, and He expressed freely. He wept. He groaned. He rejoiced. He was anguished.

This chapter is a divine permission slip: *You can feel and still be faithful.* You can limp and still lead. Below are glimpses of Jesus' emotional life and what each one teaches us about navigating leadership and life with grace.

1. **Grief – "Jesus Wept." (John 11:35)** Jesus wept openly at the tomb of Lazarus, even knowing resurrection was moments away. Why? Because grief is not weakness, it is love refusing to let go.

Reflection: *What are you grieving that you haven't given yourself permission to feel?*

2. **Overwhelm – "His sweat was like drops of blood." (Luke 22:44)** In Gethsemane, Jesus didn't suppress His distress. He prayed through it. He felt the full weight of His calling and chose surrender over suppression.

Reflection: *What pressure are you carrying that needs to be released in prayer, not performance?*

3. **Anger – "He overturned the tables." (Mark 11:15-17)** Jesus responded with righteous indignation to injustice and corruption. His anger wasn't reckless; it was purposeful.

Reflection: *What injustice are you called to confront without apology?*

4. **Joy – "Jesus, full of joy through the Holy Spirit…" (Luke 10:21)** Joy wasn't absent in Jesus' ministry. He celebrated, connected, and delighted in obedience and revelation.

Reflection: *Where is joy showing up in your journey, and have you paused to embrace it?*

5. **Compassion – "He was moved with compassion…" (Matthew 9:36).** Jesus

was led by love. His miracles were often preceded by compassion, not pressure.

Reflection: *Is your leadership fueled by compassion or obligation?*

6. **Loneliness – "My God, why have You forsaken Me?" (Matthew 27:46)** Even Jesus felt abandoned. In His most painful moment, He voiced the ache of distance—and in doing so, gave us permission to do the same.

Reflection: *Where do you need to stop pretending you're fine and start being honest with God?*

Affirmation: Emotional Faithfulness I am not disqualified by my emotions. Like Jesus, I can feel fully and lead faithfully. My tears don't make me fragile—they make me honest. I give myself permission to weep, rest, rejoice, and rise. I am made in the image of a Savior who cried.

Closing Prayer: Lord, thank You for modeling emotional integrity. Thank You for showing us that tears, anger, joy, and weariness have a place in divine purpose. Help me to stop hiding my heart and start healing in Your presence. Teach me to lead with empathy, to live with emotional honesty, and to never be ashamed of my humanity. In Jesus name, amen.

Jesus wept, and so can you. Not because you are weak, but because you are walking closely with the One who feels it all too.

Reflection Journal

**Guided Prompts for the Limping Leader,
Disruptor, and Legacy Builders**

This is your space.
No pressure to be polished.
No need to impress.
Just bring your honest self to the page,
limp and all.

Question 1

When Did I Start Hiding?

Describe the moment or season when you began to shrink, perform, or protect yourself out of fear.

- What happened?
- How did it shape the way you saw yourself?
- What vow did you make in that moment that God is now asking you to break?

_____

_____

_____

_____

_____

_____

_____

_____

_____

_____

_____

_____

_____

_____

_____

_____

_____

CASSANDRA L. WILLIAMS

LEAD WITH THE LIMP

_____

_____

_____

_____

_____

_____

_____

_____

_____

_____

_____

_____

_____

_____

_____

_____

_____

_____

_____

_____

_____

_____

_____

_____

_____

_____

_____

_____

_____

_____

Question 2

What Patterns Have I Stayed Loyal To?

List the emotional, mental, or behavioral patterns you've clung to that once protected you but now imprison you.

- What are they trying to protect you from?
- What truth is God inviting you to replace them with?
- Where is He asking you to trade survival for surrender?

_____

_____

_____

_____

_____

_____

_____

_____

_____

_____

_____

_____

_____

_____

_____

_____

_____

LEAD WITH THE LIMP

Question 3

What Does Leading with the Limp Look Like for Me?

Visualize yourself leading just as you are.

- What does it feel like?
- Who benefits when you show up unapologetically?
- What part of your story have you been withholding that God is now asking you to use?

_____

_____

_____

_____

_____

_____

_____

_____

_____

_____

_____

_____

_____

_____

Question 4

Who or What Dropped Me?

Write about the experiences, people, or seasons that left you wounded.

- How have you processed that pain?
- What parts still need healing?
- What does forgiveness look like in this area, not just for them, but for you?

_____

_____

_____

_____

_____

_____

_____

_____

_____

_____

_____

_____

_____

_____

_____

_____

_____

Question 5

Where Do I Sense God Calling Me to Step Out, Even While Limping?

What space, table, room, or assignment have you delayed because you're waiting to feel "whole"?

- What would it look like to obey anyway?
- What is one bold step you can take this week to disrupt fear and step into your assignment?

_____

_____

_____

_____

_____

_____

_____

_____

_____

_____

_____

_____

_____

_____

_____

_____

_____

Question 6

What Legacy Am I Building?

If someone watched your life as a blueprint, what would they learn about leadership, faith, and authenticity?

- How do you want to be remembered?
- What part of your limp can become someone else's hope?
- What generational cycles are you called to disrupt so your legacy looks different?

_____

_____

_____

_____

_____

_____

_____

_____

_____

_____

_____

_____

_____

_____

_____

Question 7

A Raw Prayer from Me to God

Use this space to write a personal, unrehearsed prayer.

- What do you need from God in this season?
- Where are you still wrestling?
- What are you ready to release into His hands today?

God, I give You…
I trust You to…
I release…
I choose to lead with the limp because…

_____

_____

_____

_____

_____

_____

_____

_____

_____

_____

_____

_____

_____

_____

_____

CASSANDRA L. WILLIAMS

LEAD WITH THE LIMP

Tactical Grace

Support for the Limping Leader
Scripture. Strategy. Surrender.
*A practical well of wisdom for the battles
you fight behind the scenes.*

1. Comparison

Insight:
Comparison is a confidence thief. It whispers, "You're behind," while God is saying, "You're exactly where I need you." The more we stare at someone else's lane, the more we forfeit momentum in our own.

Biblical Principle:
"Let us run with perseverance the race marked out for us, fixing our eyes on Jesus…"
—Hebrews 12:1-2 (NIV)

Affirmation:
I am not behind. I am not overlooked. I am running my race with divine precision and purpose.

Prayer:
Father, forgive me for the moments I've measured my worth by someone else's progress. Help me fix my eyes on You and the path You've carved uniquely for me. I choose to run in my lane with joy, boldness, and focus. Amen.

2. Guilt

Insight:
Guilt often lingers long after the apology, the lesson, or the change. It keeps leaders second-guessing their decisions and questioning their right to move forward. But grace doesn't just forgive, it frees.

Biblical Principle:
"Therefore, there is now no condemnation for those who are in Christ Jesus..."
—Romans 8:1 (NIV)

Strategy:
Identify one lingering guilt and ask: *Is this God convicting me or the enemy condemning me?* If it's shame without instruction, it's not from Him.

Prayer:
Lord, I release the weight of what I can't undo. I receive Your grace as a covering, not a concept. Help me walk forward, not in guilt, but in gratitude for Your mercy. Amen.

3. Shame

Insight:
Shame doesn't just say you *did* something wrong, it says you *are* something wrong. It rewrites identity, not just behavior. But God has already rewritten your story in grace.

Biblical Principle:
"Instead of your shame you shall receive a double portion…"
—Isaiah 61:7 (ESV)

Affirmation:
I am not my past. I am not my failure. I am who God says I am, restored, righteous, and released from shame.

Prayer:
Jesus, thank You for taking my shame to the cross. I reject every voice that tries to label me by my lowest moments. Wrap me in Your truth until shame no longer speaks louder than grace. Amen.

4. Frustration

Insight:
Frustration is often a sign that your soul is trying to lead from a place it hasn't had time to rest, recover, or release. It's not failure, it's feedback.

Biblical Principle:
"Be still before the Lord and wait patiently for him…"
—Psalm 37:7 (NIV)

Strategy:
Pause. Don't react. Ask, "What is this frustration trying to reveal?" Let the tension become a teacher, not a trigger.

Prayer:
Father, calm the storm within me. Help me pause before I push, pray before I plan, and surrender before I speak. I release the pressure and receive Your peace. Amen.

5. Insecurity

Insight:
Insecurity whispers that you're not enough. Not smart enough. Not spiritual enough. Not strong enough. But God never asked you to lead from your own strength; He asked you to trust His.

Biblical Principle:
"But he said to me, 'My grace is sufficient for you, for my power is made perfect in weakness.'"
—2 Corinthians 12:9 (NIV)

Affirmation:
I am not called to be perfect; I am called to be present. God's grace fills every gap my confidence cannot.

Prayer:
Lord, where I feel small, stretch my belief in Your ability. I release the lies of inadequacy and step into the strength that comes from being Yours. Let Your confidence anchor my calling. Amen.

6. Lack of Boundaries

Insight:
When you're wired to serve, boundaries can feel like betrayal. But boundaries aren't rejection, they're protection. They preserve your assignment and guard your peace.

Biblical Principle:
"Let what you say be simply 'Yes' or 'No'; anything more than this comes from evil."
—Matthew 5:37 (ESV)

Strategy:
One sacred "no" can create room for the right "yes." Identify where you're overcommitted and ask: *What am I protecting by saying no?*

Prayer:
Father, give me courage to honor the space You've called me to steward. Teach me that saying no to people is sometimes saying yes to You. Strengthen my "no" and bless my "yes." Amen.

7. Being Misunderstood

Insight:
You were called to be clear, not always to be accepted. Being misunderstood comes with the weight of leadership, especially when you're called to disrupt norms others aren't ready to release.

Biblical Principle:
"The stone the builders rejected has become the cornerstone."
—Psalm 118:22 (NIV)

Affirmation:
My worth is not measured by being understood; my assignment is affirmed by obedience.

Prayer:
God, remind me that You were misunderstood, too. Anchor me in clarity even when others question my motives. Let me find peace in Your affirmation, not public approval. Amen.

8. Encountering Bullies & Mean People

Insight:
Even in ministry and leadership, mean-spirited people will try to intimidate, manipulate, or silence you. But you are not called to match their energy, you're called to model Kingdom authority.

Biblical Principle:
"Do not be overcome by evil, but overcome evil with good."
—Romans 12:21 (NIV)

Strategy:
Stay rooted in identity. Respond from wholeness, not woundedness. You don't have to defend yourself when heaven already does.

Prayer:
Father, protect my heart from bitterness and my tongue from retaliation. When I encounter dishonor, help me respond with dignity. Cover me with courage to confront, wisdom to discern, and grace to walk away when needed. Amen.

9. Imposter Syndrome

Insight:
You're in the room, but something inside keeps asking, *"Who let me in?"* Imposter syndrome isn't humility, it's sabotage. It causes you to question what God already confirmed.

Biblical Principle:
"Not that we are competent in ourselves... but our competence comes from God."
—2 Corinthians 3:5 (NIV)

Affirmation:
I am not an imposter, I am anointed. I didn't sneak in. God sent me.

Prayer:
God, silence the voice of false humility that questions my place in the spaces You've assigned me to. Help me walk in quiet confidence, knowing I am equipped, empowered, and endorsed by You. Amen.

10. Leadership Fatigue

Insight:
Even visionaries get tired. Leading, pouring, showing up again and again while still bleeding behind the scenes can leave you spiritually dehydrated. Fatigue isn't failure, it's a signal to refuel.

Biblical Principle:
"Come to me, all who are weary and burdened, and I will give you rest."
—Matthew 11:28 (NIV)

Strategy:
Rest is not optional; it's obedience. Schedule sacred rest without apology.

Prayer:
Father, I give You the weight of everything I've been carrying. Refresh me where I've grown weary. Restore my joy, renew my energy, and remind me that even leaders need rest. Amen.

11. Ministry & Marriage Tension

Insight:
Sometimes the hardest place to lead is at home. Balancing ministry and marriage can leave you pulled, misunderstood, and carrying the emotional load for everyone. But leadership doesn't have to cost your covenant.

Biblical Principle:
"Two are better than one… If either of them falls down, one can help the other up."
—Ecclesiastes 4:9-10 (NIV)

Affirmation:
My marriage is not my obstacle; it's my ministry. I choose unity, not silent resentment.

Prayer:
Lord, bless our rhythm. Help me prioritize partnership over performance. Heal what's unspoken, soften what's hardened, and make our marriage a safe place again. Use us, not just individually, but as a team, for Your glory. Amen.

12. Grieving While Leading

Insight:
Grief doesn't pause your assignment, but it does weigh on your soul. Leading while grieving is heavy, but God is present in the ache.

Biblical Principle:
"The Lord is close to the brokenhearted and saves those who are crushed in spirit."
—Psalm 34:18 (NIV)

Affirmation:
I can mourn and still move forward. Grief does not disqualify me; it draws me closer to God.

Prayer:
Jesus, thank You for weeping with me. I bring You the loss I can't explain and the tears I try to hide. Hold me as I heal. Give me grace to keep leading without pretending I'm not hurting. Amen.

13. Delay: When the Wait Becomes a Weight

Insight:
Waiting on God can be holy, but when the wait stretches long, it can feel like a burden instead of a blessing. Delay starts to sound like denial, and hope starts to feel heavy. But God isn't just working *for* you in the delay; He's working *in* you.

Biblical Principle:
"Hope deferred makes the heart sick, but a longing fulfilled is a tree of life."
—Proverbs 13:12 (NIV)

Affirmation:
This delay is not my denial. I will not despise the wait, God is stretching me for what I prayed for.

Prayer:
God, I trust You even when I don't understand the pace. Help me carry the wait without losing my hope. Anchor me in promise, not pain. Strengthen me to grow in the dark while You prepare the light. Amen.

14. Spiritual Dryness

Insight:
Even when you love God, there are seasons where the well feels dry. Prayer feels forced. Worship feels routine. But dryness doesn't mean distance—sometimes it's the invitation to deeper dependency.

Biblical Principle:
"O God, you are my God; earnestly I seek you… in a dry and parched land where there is no water."
—Psalm 63:1 (NIV)

Affirmation:
Even when I feel dry, I am not disconnected. I will seek Him anyway.

Prayer:
God, I miss feeling close to You. Quench this thirst that no platform, person, or performance can satisfy. Pull me back to the well of Your presence. Amen.

15. Loneliness in Leadership

Insight:
You're surrounded but still feel isolated. Sometimes the weight of vision can separate you from the comfort of familiarity. But even when others fall away, God never leaves.

Biblical Principle:
"At my first defense, no one came to my support… But the Lord stood at my side and gave me strength."
—2 Timothy 4:16-17 (NIV)

Affirmation:
I am not alone in this assignment. God stands with me even when others do not.

Prayer:
Lord, hold me steady when I feel unseen. Let Your nearness be more real to me than the silence of people. Surround me with the right tribe at the right time. Amen.

16. People-Pleasing

Insight:
When your worth is tied to what others think, obedience becomes compromised. You weren't called to be palatable, you were called to be prophetic.

Biblical Principle:
"Am I now trying to win the approval of human beings, or of God?"
—Galatians 1:10 (NIV)

Strategy:
Check every "yes" with heaven before offering it to people.

Prayer:
Father, break my addiction to approval. I don't want to lead for likes, I want to lead for legacy. Teach me to please You first, even if it costs me the crowd. Amen.

17. Fear of Outgrowing Your Circle

Insight:
Growth is uncomfortable, not just for you, but for those around you. But shrinking to fit old molds will choke the next version of your calling.

Biblical Principle:
"Forget the former things; do not dwell on the past. See, I am doing a new thing!"
—Isaiah 43:18-19 (NIV)

Affirmation:
I release the fear of leaving what no longer grows me. I trust God with what remains and what must shift.

Prayer:
God, help me honor my history without becoming a hostage to it. Make me brave enough to move forward without apology. Amen.

18. Unanswered Prayers

Insight:
When the prayer has gone up, but the answer still hasn't come down, the temptation is to believe God is ignoring you. But delay is not rejection. It's refinement.

Biblical Principle:
"Though it linger, wait for it; it will certainly come and will not delay."
—Habakkuk 2:3 (NIV)

Affirmation:
God heard me the first time. And He's working, even in the silence.

Prayer:
Lord, strengthen me to trust Your timeline. Let me lean into Your character when I can't see Your hand. Amen.

19. False Responsibility

Insight:
When you carry more than God assigned, you end up depleted and resentful. You are not the savior, you are the servant.

Biblical Principle:
"For my yoke is easy and my burden is light."
—Matthew 11:30 (NIV)

Strategy:
Ask daily: *Is this mine to carry, or Yours?* Release what doesn't belong on your shoulders.

Prayer:
Jesus, I lay down what isn't mine. Help me walk in alignment, not exhaustion. Remind me that obedience doesn't require over-functioning. Amen.

20. Discouragement After Obedience

Insight:
You obeyed. You trusted. And it still got harder. Just like Elijah under the broom tree, even bold prophets need rest after the breakthrough doesn't look like what they expected.

Biblical Principle:
"Elijah… came to a broom bush, sat down under it and prayed that he might die…"
—1 Kings 19:4 (NIV)

Affirmation:
Obedience is never wasted. God honors every "yes", even the heavy ones.

Prayer:
God, when obedience leaves me exhausted instead of elevated, restore my confidence in You. Remind me that results don't always come fast, but fruit always comes. Amen.

21. Fear of Being Too Much

Insight:

If you've ever been told you're too deep, too loud, or too passionate, you've likely dimmed yourself for people who couldn't handle your full shine. But your fire was never meant to be manageable; it was meant to be holy.

Biblical Principle:
"But if I say, 'I will not mention his word'… his word is in my heart like a fire… I am weary of holding it in; indeed, I cannot."
—Jeremiah 20:9 (NIV)

Affirmation:
I am not too much; I am exactly what this generation needs.

Prayer:
God, reignite what I've tried to shrink. Let me burn with holy fire; not to entertain, but to transform. Amen.

22. Wrestling with the Call

Insight:
You love God, but if you're honest, there are days when you wish He'd chosen someone else. But the call doesn't go away. It waits. And it whispers: *"You were born for this."*

Biblical Principle:
"For God's gifts and his call are irrevocable."
—Romans 11:29 (NIV)

Affirmation:
I won't run from what I was made for, even when it stretches me.

Prayer:
Father, I surrender again. Even when I wrestle with the weight of the call, help me remember why You chose me. Use my limp for Your glory. Amen.

23. Starting Over (Again)

Insight:
Starting over again can feel like failure in disguise. But every ending is a setup for reinvention. And every new beginning is a sign you're still in the story.

Biblical Principle:
"Do not despise these small beginnings…"
—Zechariah 4:10 (NLT)

Affirmation:
This is not the end of me, it's the beginning of something new in me.

Prayer:
God, give me the courage to rebuild. Breathe fresh wind into old bones. Remind me that nothing I've walked through will be wasted. Amen.

Next Steps: Your Journey Isn't Over

You've read the words. You've wrestled with the truths. You've felt the tug in your spirit.

Now it's time to walk it out; *limp and all.*

Whether you're ready to heal, grow, lead, or build, here are powerful ways to go deeper in your journey at Cassandra Williams Enterprises (www. thecassandrawilliams.com):

1:1 Coaching with Coach Williams

Work directly with me to uncover hidden patterns, embrace your limp, and activate your God-given identity. These sessions are safe, strategic spaces for women who are ready to stop shrinking and start showing up fully.

Unmasked: The Blueprint to Becoming

A transformational 6-week experience designed for high-achieving women ready to stop performing and start becoming. This is your guided path to emotional healing, spiritual renewal, and courageous authenticity.

Lead With the Limp: Mentorship Experience

A 12-week mentorship for leaders who are done hiding behind titles, trauma, or expectations. We explore identity, leadership style, spiritual formation, and legacy, empowering you to lead boldly in every area of life.

Wise Wives Build

Join a sacred sisterhood of women committed to becoming all God created them to be without losing themselves in the process. This space is honest, healing, and full of grace for wives who want to thrive emotionally, spiritually, and relationally.

The Victory Bookstore

Explore a growing collection of faith-rooted books, journals, and tools to help you live and lead with intention. Whether you're looking for a breakthrough resource or a gift that speaks life, the Victory Bookstore is your stop.

AUTHOR BIO

Coach Cassandra L. Williams
The Life Tactician™ | *Limping Leader* | *Disruptor* |
Legacy Architect

Coach Cassandra L. Williams is not your typical leader. She is a disruptor. A **Legacy Architect**. A limping leader who refuses to hide the scars that shaped her.

Known as *The Life Tactician*™, Coach Williams equips high-achieving women, weary leaders, and hidden warriors to remove the mask, reclaim their identity, and lead from a place of healing, not hiding.

With over three decades of leadership, ministry, and lived experience, she has made it her mission to challenge the status quo, flip tables where needed, and create spaces where authenticity is the norm, not the exception.

Through her bold voice, prophetic insight, and raw transparency, she teaches leaders how to stop shrinking, stop performing, and start disrupting cycles, systems, and strongholds that keep them, and those they're called to lead, bound.

In *Lead With the Limp: Born to Disrupt,* and her transformational mentorship program *Lead With the Limp: The Blueprint to Becoming Her,* Coach Williams gives women permission to stop waiting for perfect conditions and start leading now, limp, scars, and all.

She is also the founder of **Wise Wives Build**, a transformative community for women of faith who are ready to break free from loyal patterns, embrace authentic leadership, and build a legacy that outlives them.